Holiness, Holiness

Jean M. Cooper

WestBow Press books may be ordered through booksellers or by contacting:

WestBow Press
A Division of Thomas Nelson & Zondervan
1663 Liberty Drive
Bloomington, IN 47403
www.westbowpress.com
844-714-3454

ISBN: 979-8-3850-0987-9 (sc)
979-8-3850-0988-6 (e)

Library of Congress Control Number: 2023919274

Print information available on the last page.

WestBow Press rev. date: 11/16/2023

WESTBOW
PRESS
A DIVISION OF THOMAS NELSON
& ZONDERVAN

Holiness, Holiness

Oh, Holy Night ...

It may not have been exactly on December 25th,
but there was a time when Holiness came to earth like a knight on a sinking ship.

3

Holiness, Holiness!

Appearing to wisemen and shepherds, there was a night when the angels declared, "There is freedom from sin which entraps humanity like a snare."

Holiness, Holiness!

Holiness was wrapped in a manger scene, where all sacrifices are birthed.
He came to give us all new life and a second chance here on earth.

Holiness, Holiness!

The angels then came to Joseph to warn him in a dream,
telling them to run to a place they had never seen.

9

Holiness, Holiness!

The soldiers came through the city that night
and killed every baby boy under two in their sight.

The stomping of soldiers' feet was all the
people heard because of the jealousy in
King Herod's heart was so absurd.

11

Holiness, Holiness!

Through the cries of dear mothers' fears, one little baby boy was saved, through many mothers' tears.

Holiness, Holiness!

Holiness is who He was.

He volunteered from Heaven just because.

15

Holiness, Holiness!

Holiness was born to bring us all a gift...
A new life, if we would believe in Him just a little bit.

17

Holiness, Holiness!

As you unwrap your gifts, please remember this one you were given.
Holiness is who He was in the manger, sent for all of us to be forgiven.

Definition of holiness – state of being holy.

"a life of holiness and total devotion to God"

Through having faith and loving Jesus who made this all possible,

Holiness, Holiness is quite attainable and virtually unstoppable.

John 3:16 For God so loved the world, that he gave his only begotten Son, that whosoever believeth in him should not perish, but have everlasting life. KJV

Printed in the United States
by Baker & Taylor Publisher Services